T0114742

THE TAO Within

MING WU, PH.D.

AND

JUDY LIN

BALBOA.PRESS
A DIVISION OF HAY HOUSE

Balboa Press books may be ordered through booksellers or by contacting:

Balboa Press
A Division of Hay House
1663 Liberty Drive
Bloomington, IN 47403
www.balboapress.com
844-682-1282

Print information available on the last page.

ISBN: 979-8-7652-4783-9 (sc)
ISBN: 979-8-7652-4784-6 (e)

Library of Congress Control Number: 2023922817

Balboa Press rev. date: 12/04/2023

Dedication

This book is dedicated to all individuals who seek the divine truth of the mind–body–spirit connection. It is about discovering our innate healing powers and natural intelligence. We need true health and well-being to enjoy this existence called life.

We share this book with those who have endured immense health issues and suffering, with those who seek recovery, and with those who seek longevity and a sustainable lifestyle. We offer another perspective on healthcare and the alternative option of Taoist Chinese Medicine.

We dedicate this book to those who want to learn more about the Taoist Way and incorporate a lifestyle that embraces spirit, nature and self-awareness.

Take your power back!

Contents

Preface: The Spirit Speaks

In each one of us, there is divinity.

We are souls of infinite power, with the wisdom to create, to heal and to manifest our reality to the fullest extent of our capabilities. We can discover the essence of who we are and who we can become through our learnings and our spiritual practice, because we are spiritual beings first and foremost. Our physical bodies can be repaired when we utilize our healing energies.

Inside all of us, there is an innate intelligence that can heal itself when given the right resources and when spared unnecessary interferences. Our bodies are designed to self-repair, but our current medical system does not promote sustainable health and instead seeks to profit from illness as its first priority.

The spirit to heal and receive healing is embedded in Eastern health practices. These practices focus on the whole body/mind/spirit interconnection and its entwined presence within our social and environmental surroundings. Generally, mainstream Western medicine and its practicing physicians do not see this perspective as necessary or desirable in the diagnosis and treatment of illness, nor in the maintenance of a healthy equilibrium between body, mind and spirit. Western medicine does not acknowledge the soul in general.

The core focus and strength of the Western medical paradigm is the isolation of a problem with a potential or likely diagnosis based upon symptoms, patient history, physical examination, tests, research-based treatment options, and so on. However, this core focus generally excludes emotional and spiritual considerations.

This book's intention is to offer a new perspective and explore an alternative medical model that is missing in Western medicine, called Taoist Chinese Medicine.

Taoist Chinese Medicine (TCM) is about knowing yourself and taking your power back.

It teaches us about how to balance the body with a vital life force, or 'Qi', that is circulated in our meridian channels and organ channels. TCM practices and treatments seek to bring about the physical, mental and spiritual conditions for optimal health. TCM taps into the infinite energetic power inside all of us. Its purpose is to treat the unique constitution and genetics of a person, beyond what is seen in the conventional and biomedical sense. TCM treats the whole person, embracing each individual's emotional makeup and their energetic types of yin and yang, following the natural laws of the universe.

This book is the beginning of a journey towards knowing oneself. Self-healing is a vital part of becoming whole. Our bodies are essentially bioelectric systems that give us information about our overall health and well-being. The ancient TCM is the oldest, most profound healing practice, dating back 1,750 years. When our Qi or life force is flowing unencumbered by emotional blockages or any energy blockages, we remain in excellent health and harmony.

Dr. Ming Wu (Ph.D.), founder and doctor of Fengyang Taoist Chinese Medicine, is a doctor who treats more than the physical body. He teaches and guides his patients to help them understand that our bodies are more than just physical matter. Our spirit, our emotions and our thoughts have direct impact on the body. We learn how positive or negative emotions can lead our bodies into a state of excellent health and balance, or a trajectory of decline and disease. Dr. Wu's medical practice focuses on understanding the root cause of an ailment and seeks to address it once and for all, putting faith in the principles of TCM and applying them with patience, rather than seeking a temporary fix or a momentary recovery. While many people now understand these principles, there remains a disconnect with our current healthcare system. Why are people being let down despite all our medical advancements and technology for treatments?

THE CURRENT
HEALTHCARE SYSTEM

Americans are getting sicker.

People are feeling hopeless and suffering more than they need to.

The current medical system in the U.S. is designed to keep you on a medication treadmill. Doctors are not communicating seamlessly with other specialists in order to to see the whole picture of the patient they are treating.

Some have just suffered enough. Privately, people discuss the medical abuse they've endured and the threats they've received when they have questioned doctors about what they are doing. The Western medical system does not support a sustainable life.

Healthcare insurance premiums continue to skyrocket each year by between 2 and 5%, and that's not including out-of-pocket costs. There is no end in sight in the ongoing prescription drug crisis, which defines the norm: pharmaceuticals remain the answer to all ailments without addressing the root cause. Pop the pill and continue on the drug treadmill for decades and, most likely, the rest of your life. Is that what you want?

Rural areas have less access to healthcare services and hospitals. The abuse of prescription opioids is leading some patients to addiction. But pain is not only treatable with pills only; by understanding the entire patient journey and identifying the root cause of the pain, a holistic approach to treating pain is possible.

There are several factors, present before and since the COVID-19 pandemic, that deserve consideration in our global healthcare crisis.

Key issues include:

1. Access to care: many people still lack access to inexpensive and inclusive healthcare. Some simply cannot access the care they need due to their location or personal circumstances, which results in illnesses going untreated and worsening situations.
2. Increasing healthcare costs: healthcare costs and premiums are increasing globally, making it harder for people to afford critical care and to keep up with premiums.
3. Demographic disparities: factors including race, age, gender, sexual orientation, socioeconomic status and disability status are linked to health inequities, as some communities do not have the access to healthcare or local hospitals and continue to experience high rates of sickness.
4. Aging populations: improvements in healthcare services for the elderly are needed urgently as an increasing proportion of people live on into old age.
5. Ongoing and future pandemics: COVID-19 had an impact on healthcare systems all across the world, and innovation is required into the future to help medical services handle the ongoing challenges relating to the pandemic.

Overall, the predicament facing the healthcare system is complex. One certainty is that new resources need to be invested in order to ensure the provision of high-quality, affordable services.

American healthcare is undeniably a highly fractured system where bureaucracy, monopoly and the "powers that be" have supreme control over provision and health outcomes.

How can we fix this and resurrect the concept of people's sovereign right to good health, and remove the need to pound the commercial treadmill of government-mandated laws and ever-spiraling costs?

Professor Erin C. Fuse Brown of Georgia State University's College of Law described the predicament of the country's commercialized healthcare service, saying: "Spiraling prescription drug costs are another largely unresolved yet pressing issue. When the U.S. Food & Drug Administration (FDA) approves a new drug, it also grants the pharmaceutical company the exclusive right to market the drug for several years. This creates a monopoly."[1]

We are in the battle of the century. It is a battle for our well-being, our mental health, our physical health and our spiritual health, all while living in a modern society that sets people up to become consumers in a system that does not have their best interests at heart.

We all want a life of longevity, and for our bodies and minds to carry us into old age. We need good health in order to do so, and not to feel encumbered by immobility, pain, disease or dysfunctions. Aging gracefully is something most of us hope for, and that means sustaining a healthy body, mind and spirit that allow us to function, live, play and enjoy life.

II

THE PROS AND CONS OF
WESTERN MEDICINE

Pros

Western medicine, commonly referred to as allopathic medicine, is a school of medicine that emphasizes the use of contemporary medical approaches like medications, surgery and radiation therapy to diagnose, cure and prevent illness. It is founded on the scientific method.

It has revolutionized healthcare by bringing a rigorous scientific approach to the study and treatment of illness, and by continuously advancing medical knowledge and technology to improve patient outcomes.

In this way, Western medicine has produced the following significant benefits:

1. **Science-based medicine and evidence-based medicine:** Western medicine is anchored in rigorous scientific research and evidence-based practices, which have led to new treatments and therapies that are highly effective and safe.
2. **Specialization:** Western medicine doctors can specialize in specific areas of medicine, such as cardiology, neurology and oncology, which can aid in personalized treatments for patients.
3. **Technology:** With the rise of AI (artificial intelligence) and current technology, such as imaging equipment, robotic surgery, and other innovations, the way medicine is practiced will be

more precise, with the capacity to conduct more complex surgeries. These advances have already led to improved accuracy and outcomes in many medical procedures.

4. **Disease prevention:** From a Western medical perspective, significant strides have been made in disease prevention, through screening programs for cancer and other diseases, as well as the use of vaccines.

5. **Public health:** Western medicine has played a crucial role in improving public health, such as through sanitation and hygiene practices, and the development of public health policies and programs.

6. **Emergency situations:** Western medicine is used most effectively to save lives. It has also produced a wide range of technologies that allow for accurate diagnosis and data for many health conditions in emergency situations, such as diagnostic tools like MRI and CT scans. For injured patients, going to the emergency room is the best option in urgent care situations that require serious and immediate care. Medical institutions and hospitals can diagnose medical problems within a few hours thanks to the use of laboratories, X-Rays and other procedures.

7. **The band aid effect:** modern medications can quickly alleviate most negative symptoms to allow people to resume their daily lives with minimal interruption or discomfort. For instance, some ibuprofen could quickly clear up a headache, while tailored medicines clear up the symptoms of colds, flu, sore throats and so on. However, development and availability of such a wide range of pharmaceutical products has led to one of Western medicine's disadvantages: drug abuse.

Cons

While Western medicine has made positive contributions, it also has its drawbacks.

1. **Isolated diagnostics**: The core problem is that most traditional Western medicine treats the symptoms of a health problem and

isolates its origin. When a generalist doctor cannot fix the patient's ailment, they are referred to a specialist who carries out yet more analysis and diagnostics before possibly transferring the patient on to other specialists. Every specialist is working in silo and not communicating or working together to nail down the original problem or root cause of the patient's health condition. The process tends to focus on treating symptoms rather than addressing the root cause of an illness. To improve treatment, there should be a collaborative communication structure through which primary doctors can talk to specialists, as part of the medical model.

2. **Top-tier vs. low-tier doctors:** In Western culture or the U.S., the top-tier medical doctors are the last you see when your symptoms have progressed and escalated to an emergency situation. In Eastern cultures like China, patients see the top-tier medical doctors right away, to address the problem and to prevent it from developing into a disease that becomes untreatable. An analogy for the Eastern approach is to think of the patient as a rock that has slipped and is falling down a hill. While Western medicine focuses on the outcome, or waits to see what the rock will hit, Eastern doctors want to eliminate the problem by stopping the rock in its tracks and preventing it from slipping any further. Eastern medicine seeks to nip the root cause before the health condition worsens.

3. **High costs**: Western medicine can be costly, making it inaccessible for many people who cannot afford medical treatment or keep up with the rising healthcare premiums.

4. **Side effects & long-term effects:** Western medicine often relies on pharmaceuticals, which can have negative side effects for patients and enable drug abuse and addiction. Medications can weigh heavily on the body in the later years of a person's life. Overuse of antidepressants and mood stabilizers can cause a tremendous amount of damage to a person's organs over prolonged periods. Some medications interact harmfully with other substances found in everyday consumables.

5. **Invasive treatments:** Western medicine has been criticized for being too invasive, leading to unnecessary surgeries or treatments.

While modern medicine has given the world a science-based and evidence-based approach to healthcare, it often fails to see patients as a whole person and acknowledge the broader picture of each individual's human experience. Modern medicine has also been exploited by organizations and companies that see people as commodities for making money.

While the medical component of treatment for health problems is essential, it is easy to neglect the internal and external factors that have a bearing on an individual's life. Acknowledging these factors requires attention on two areas of experience.

Internal and External Factors of Health Problems

The root causes of health problems can be broadly divided into two categories: internal factors and external factors.

1. **Internal:** Our emotional makeup has an impact on the internal ecosystem and chemistry of our bodies. Stress or emotional disharmony caused by the strains of modern life, family, work and the world at large can be absorbed, causing harm to our bodies.
2. **External:** Environmental impacts, such as pesticides, toxic exposure or toxins ingested, can also take their toll on our bodies. Our environment is in a state of imbalance and jeopardy. Climate change has impacted our weather and water sources, disrupting the natural flow of life and the ecosystem. Our air is polluted by airborne chemicals. Our foods are affected by toxins and pesticides, and the water in many of our cities is contaminated.

These internal and external factors hold clues to where many ailments begin and how they manifest into our physical beings before spiraling within the context of our collapsing healthcare system that fails to address the root cause of diseases.

Overall, while Western medicine has its strengths, it is important to consider both the advantages and limitations when deciding on a healthcare approach.

III

MEDICAL TECHNOLOGY LACKS DEFINITIVE ANSWERS TO HEALTH PROBLEMS

With all of our advanced medical technology, why are people still struggling with disease and chronic illnesses?

This is the 'holy grail' of all questions in the field. With all the developments that have been made to shape the landscape of healthcare in the 21st century, one could be forgiven for hoping that medical institutions would have established ways to manage chronic illnesses in a productive, healthy, balanced way, instead of regressing patients and relying on prescription medication to address pain. In short, the medical system is making Americans sicker.

Chronic illnesses and diseases are often complex conditions that cannot be easily explained, diagnosed or treated. The multi-factorial origins of these conditions contribute to the ongoing struggle to find adequate medical responses to them. Modern medicine seeks answers by treating symptoms, which can alleviate problems temporarily, but when genetic, environmental and lifestyle factors all contribute to a condition, alternative approaches are required.

Modern lifestyles often contributed to conditions such as heart disease, diabetes and obesity. People struggling with these conditions may require help in making changes to their diet, in managing stress, or in changing their environment, all of which can be difficult to achieve and sustain.

Low-income and underserved communities may not have access to preventative care or early intervention, leading to more advanced and difficult-to-treat diseases. In some rural areas, there are very limited medical resources, leaving patients facing a journey of two hours or more to reach their nearest hospital.

There are limits to the solutions our current healthcare system can provide, as well as difficulties regarding its accessibility for many patients. The system is also aligned firmly with Western approaches to medicine. Many specialists push their standard protocols onto patients as a "one-size-fits-all" approach, when in reality each individual's history, biology, environment and lifestyle should be explored in order to provide tailored treatment plans.

When the COVID-19 crisis hit, vaccines were mandated in work environments, school systems, hospitals and more. Many who were called upon to take the vaccine faced the choice of doing so or losing their jobs. Questions remain over the lack of transparency in the vaccine program and the failure to disclose the composition of the vaccines themselves. Government mandates were broadly accepted and people were required to show proof of vaccinations when traveling, while pharmaceutical companies like Moderna, Pfizer and Johnson & Johnson were given protection from liability in the event that people experienced adverse reactions or side effects after being given the vaccines.[2]

Part of knowing who you are is to know your body and what you put in it. We typically do not do enough homework or due diligence before accepting medical orders. The healthcare system has been monopolized and uses our bodies as commodities for profit.

Recognition is growing in the West that health is not just the absence of disease, but a state of physical, mental and social well-being. According to this view, promoting good health among populations requires a more holistic and integrative approach to healthcare, which addresses not just the physical symptoms of disease, but also the emotional, social and environmental factors that contribute to overall health and well-being.

While medical technology has made significant strides in the diagnosis and treatment of many diseases, addressing the root causes of illness requires a more comprehensive approach, including lifestyle modifications, preventative care and addressing social determinants of health.

The neglect of the spirit in our body is a major problem and cause of ailments. Spirit is the essence of our being, but it is overlooked by Western medicine. By recognizing the spirit or energies in the body, we can integrate natural healing powers by harmonizing our TCM treatment with spirit. Clinical studies have produced results that demonstrate the efficacy of practices like Qi Gong and Tai Chi in treating conditions like anxiety and depression, and their benefits in emotional regulation.[3]

The focus of medical doctors is concentrated on the patient's physical condition, their symptoms and the necessary medicinal treatment of the individual. Recovery is achieved in the physical, three-dimensional sense, while the spiritual aspect is typically completely absent. In traditional terms, Western medicine's core strength is the diagnosis and treatment of disease or dysfunction at a micro-level. The Western approach entails isolating the problem at the cellular level of a specific organ or even of the patient's DNA microbiology.

We can be open to other ways of seeing and caring for the body, rather than relying on conventional Western medicine that goes largely unquestioned and unscrutinized. Knowledge is power and wisdom is making the right choices for a better life. We can discern what is best for our whole being by treating the whole person for longevity, sustainability and true health.

The alternative medical option is Taoist Chinese Medicine (TCM). Cultural differences and limited integration and education in the West have restricted the growth of TCM as a modality, and it does not align with the rigorous scientific standards of modern mainstream medicine. Misinformation has also contributed to a lack of exploration of the efficacy of TCM, despite evidence that holistic approaches to healing can provide benefits often lacking in Western approaches. However, TCM has a long history of practice and it is deeply entwined in the lives and well-being of many more people in other parts of the world.

IV

INTRODUCTION TO TAOIST CHINESE MEDICINE: AN ANCIENT PRACTICE OF OVER 1,750 YEARS

The Essence of Taoism

Taoism is an ancient philosophy of spirituality and a way of life from ancient China. The writings and beliefs at its heart came from a mystical figure named Lao Tzu, who lived 2,500 years ago. The core belief is that 'Tao' is the origin and law of all things in the universe. The Tao is "the way" and represents the natural order and flow of the universe, which is defined by balance and harmony in oneself, with nature and with others.

It emphasizes the importance of living in harmony with nature and its cycle of life, and accepting the world as it is. Another key Taoist concept is acceptance of the natural order of human existence: birth, growth, maturity, old age and death. The philosophy of Taoism embraces aging, encouraging people to welcome the cycles of life gracefully, rather than attempting to fight against them or to strive for perfection.

In modern society, there is a tendency to resist the natural process of aging by looking for solutions that can reverse time and give us back what we had in our 20s and 30s. Anti-aging creams, plastic surgery and medical spa skin treatments are examples of the products society offers towards these ends. Taoist teachings encourage acceptance and promote the value of going with the flow. Simplicity, patience, compassion, humility and non-action or "wu wei" are other core beliefs in Taoism that seek to reduce the pressures of life's challenges, particularly during times of hardship. It is then when it is most important to maintain your core and your balance.

The goal of life is to find one's own way to the rhythm of the natural world, and not to be confined by modern standards and rigidities, such as Confucian moralism, class prejudice, aggression, competition and pragmatism.

To be a part of the Tao is to unite and tune in with the universal mind and harmonize with nature by balancing the yin and yang energies. Tao is form in the formless. We can create, generate and embrace the Qi through practices like Qi Gong, Tai Chi or meditation.

The human body is an energy source that can be tapped into, because therein lies its own healing power or Qi for the body's systems. If we can integrate the mindset and practice of Taoism in our lives, we are better equipped to handle the stresses and even physical ailments that may arise during our lifetimes.

This infinite power resides in us, but we have yet to discover its magnificence and fully harness the potential healing power that is the essence of who we are as human and spiritual beings.

Cultural Perspectives Between Eastern and Western Medicine

Taoism is a broadly embraced philosophical and spiritual fabric within Chinese culture, and wider society in the East. The philosophy offers an understanding of the workings of human nature and human health in relation to nature and the universe. Taoist thinking understands and accepts that all medicinal properties can be found in nature alone, and can tap into our own internal healing powers. When we align our physical health with the inner workings of the spirit, nature and plants, it enhances our innate ability to heal by using the proper herbs and plants.

In China, herbal medicine is seen as a respected ancient Chinese medical modality and is covered by health insurance, whereas in the U.S., pharmaceutical prescriptions are paid by health insurance. This, in itself, is foretelling of the contrasting cultural perspectives on medicine and treatment of the body. TCM upholds a belief in the natural remedies found in nature, with herbs, plants and minerals viewed as gifts from the earth and that possess medicinal properties. These plants and herbs, which occur naturally in the earth, can help to restore and rejuvenate the body. In contrast, Western medicine uses technology, synthetics, pharmaceuticals, diagnostics and image scans to identify, diagnose and treat ailments in the body.

Even with all the new technologies available, medical advancement has its limits. Modern medicine misses an essential component, which is the spiritual and emotional makeup of a person.

The Taoist practice is not only a cultural perspective on ancient Chinese philosophy and medicine, but also a way of life that connects with everything. It incorporates a profound knowledge of soul power and emotional makeup of the individual that can either positively or negatively impact the body.

Even in Eastern medicine, it is important to distinguish between what constitutes a legitimate practice and what constitute the classical and modern forms of Chinese medicine. Chinese medicine has split into classical and modern schools as a result of modernization. These days, modern Chinese medicine is saturated with fads and trends that prioritize making money over helping people.

The Stanford Encyclopedia of Philosophy offers the following definition: "Chinese medicine could in principle refer to: (1) the full range of medical systems used in contemporary China, including Western biomedicine; (2) the traditional indigenous Chinese medicine that is conventionally referred to as Traditional Chinese Medicine (TCM); and

(3) other indigenous medical systems, distinct from but TCM, practiced by non-Chinese or minorities who live in areas that historically were part of China or are now part of the Peoples Republic of China, for example, Korean and Tibetan medicine."[4]

TCM is a modality that offers natural healing through the integration of soul, mind and body, and has a long-standing tradition for treating the whole person. Books such as *The Way of Chuang Tzu* by Thomas Merton and the classic Chinese text *Tao Te Ching* offer an introduction to the way Taoism harnesses TCM to harmonize healing with spirituality, in the pursuit of immortality that can be achieved by eliminating disease.

The Way of the Tao is to Follow Nature

In Taoism, positions are given to the four great powers in the universe. Those four greats are: the Sovereign, the Earth, Heaven and Tao.

Chapter 25 of the Tao Te Ching describes how humans follow the laws of Earth, while Earth follows the laws of Heaven, and Heaven follows the laws of Tao. Tao, it crucially states, follows itself – that is to say it takes after what is natural.

From here, we receive the essential Taoist concept that nature is part of the essence of Tao, which is deeply rooted in all that is natural.

The Capitalism of Western Medicine

The current Western medicine model has lost sight of its true purpose and has become inherently capitalistic or profit-seeking. Since the late 19th century, industrialization, scientific advancements and corporate interests have influenced the evolution of healthcare and the Western medical system.

These influences have shaped Western medicine and produced a healthcare system that functions in a similar way to many other profit-driven, capitalistic industries. Evidence of the ways in which Western medicine is in the grips of capitalism can be found in the private healthcare systems that operate in many Western countries, whereby healthcare providers exist for the primary purpose of making profits and maximizing their returns to shareholders. Patients, rather than being the first consideration of those delivering healthcare, are viewed as consumers and often face spiraling costs to access the care they need.

Further evidence of Western medicine's positioning within a capitalist framework can be found by examining the workings of the pharmaceutical industry. The West turns to large pharmaceutical companies to research, develop, test and patent new drugs that form crucial elements of the treatment delivered by healthcare providers. These pharmaceutical companies are themselves driven by profit, which means that patients in need of healthcare ultimately have to foot the bill for their treatment in countries like the United States, where the cost of drugs is significantly higher than in many other parts of the world.[5]

Private health insurance is a key part of Western healthcare systems like the one found in the United States, where insurance companies act as intermediaries between patients and healthcare providers. Like the pharmaceutical companies, private health insurers are driven by profit and those profits are built on the premiums that people have to pay to ensure they can afford the care they need.

A reliance on innovation and advanced technology contributes to the problem of access to Western healthcare. While many positive breakthroughs have been achieved through the West's focus on using innovative approaches and modern technology to produce healthcare solutions, these developments often come at a high cost that is inevitably passed on to patients, who are viewed as consumers.

A key tenet of the capitalist system is the power of competition to produce a greater variety and higher quality of good and services for people to access. When this is applied to hospitals, clinics and medical practices, as it is in many Western countries including the United States, the result is an environment where healthcare deliverers compete for patients who can afford the most expensive care or have the most comprehensive insurance coverage, while leaving others underserved.

It is important that any critique of the Western healthcare system, while acknowledging the advances it continues to make in the development of innovative new treatments and approaches, highlights the growing disparities in access to care being driven by the profit-oriented nature of the system.

How are Prescription Drugs Created?

When pharmaceutical companies invest in research and development for new prescription drugs, future profits are at the forefront of their plans and considerations.[6]

The drugs in which those companies invest most heavily are the drugs that can generate the highest profits. Calculations are made pertaining to a given drug's expected lifetime global revenue, which will depend on factors such as the policies that affect the supply and demand for the drug. If a particular drug is not expected to be as profitable as others, it will not receive the investment it needs in order to be developed – even if there are patients who require it.

This is in stark contrast to a medical paradigm where treatments are grown and produced naturally in the wild. In herbalism, nature is the producer and we are the consumers with the responsibility to cultivate our own treatments, ensuring each person is able to take from the natural world the medicines they require.

The disparity between these approaches is clear, and at its heart is the presence or absence of Qi, or life force. Herbalism cultivates medicines in a manner that preserves the life force or Qi of all living things, which remains embedded in the plants. Pharmaceutical companies do not take this same care when producing pills in factory conditions.

Harmonizing the body with the life force of all living things offers a pathway to excellent health. When we eat living things such as plants, we absorb the live energy source contained within. Taoism welcomes this kind of thinking and a lifestyle where we are in tune with the natural cycle of life and death.

Taoism nurtures life and provides a lifestyle that integrates spirituality, a positive mindset and emotions, nutrition, fitness, keen awareness of self and others, and a way of living in harmony with society and with nature.

Western medicine all too often does not delve into the root causes of health problems, and fails to adequately acknowledge the relationships between the body, mind and spirit. The strength of Western medicine is isolating and identifying the area of the body that is in pain. In this way, the spiritual approach of Eastern medicine and the physical approach of Western medicine are in contrast to one another, and this is reflected in the long-term effects experiences by individuals in the healing process.

The cultural differences between Eastern and Western medicine are fundamental. These differences begin with the way illness is viewed, and this starting position shapes the approach taken by health practitioners. In the East, healthcare is viewed through the spiritual eyes of Taoism, and practices such as Qi Gong encourage respect for the Qi – the essence and life force that keeps us alive. Knowing how to activate the life force through movement and nutrition will promote homeostasis and stave off illness.

Western medicine is excellent at assessing and fixing the symptomology of an individual, while Eastern medicine focuses less on symptoms and instead seeks to identify the root cause of an ailment within a more holistic view of a person.

Ultimately, a key difference between the two approaches can be seen in the way Eastern medicine aims to heal patients for the long term by seeking a holistic cure, whereas Western medicine focuses on the cessation of symptoms. The latter is more open to the use of pharmaceuticals, which are often effective in addressing symptoms quickly, but do not always address the root cause of the ailment and can also lead to an unhealthy dependence on prescription drugs.

What is Qi and How Does it Relate to the Human Body?

In Taoist Chinese Medicine, Qi (pronounced "chee") is the vital life force or energy that flows through the body, enlivening and nourishing all living things. Qi circulates through the body along pathways called meridians, and its flow can be affected by internal and external factors such as emotions, diet, movement and environment.

The body is mapped by multiple meridian channels that carry Qi, to help regulate blood and the flow of essential substances throughout the body. Just as nature has rivers, channels, wastes and fluidity in waterways, our bodies function in a similar way. Our bodies' waterways involve the circulation of blood and Qi. Taoist belief is that Qi must flow and create physiological circulation continuously, otherwise stagnation may occur and cause illness. Having Qi in the body is the difference between a live body and a dead body. It is the essence of being alive and, therefore, movement is life. A core concept of Qi is that immaterial happenings (emotions) of the body can slowly become material, and manifest in the body as illness or good health.

According to TCM, maintaining the smooth and balanced flow of Qi is essential for maintaining overall health and well-being. When Qi is flowing smoothly, the body is able to function optimally, with all organs and systems working in harmony. When Qi is disrupted or blocked, however, it can lead to physical, emotional and mental imbalances, which can progress into disease and illness.

There are many practices in TCM that are designed to promote the smooth flow of Qi and maintain overall health. These include acupuncture, herbal medicine, dietary therapy, Qi Gong (a form of exercise and meditation), and Tui Na massage. Each of these practices aims to promote the flow of Qi, remove blockages, and restore balance to the body.

Research has shown that practices such as acupuncture and Qi Gong may have a number of health benefits, such as reducing stress and anxiety, improving immune function, and reducing pain and inflammation.[7] By promoting the smooth flow of Qi and maintaining overall balance and harmony in the body, TCM can help to support optimal health and well-being.

When we fix the spiritual body by practicing Qi Gong or Tai Chi, we are feeding the soul, mind and body. When Qi becomes low, the "monkey mind" awakens and can lead us into feeling defeated, depressed and full of anxiety. It is important to take care of our Qi, or "life force"; it is what is keeping us alive. When the Qi disappears entirely, you die.

V

HOW EMOTIONS IMPACT
OUR BODIES

In Taoist Chinese Medicine, there is a belief that emotions under prolonged experience can affect the health of the organs and their corresponding meridians. When we suppress our emotions for long periods of time, we can cause dysfunction. Here are the seven emotions and the organs they are associated with:

1. Joy/happiness – heart: The heart houses the shen, which is the emotional center of the body. TCM tells us that the joy and happiness we experience is closely linked to the health of the heart. A healthy heart promotes these positive emotions, according to TCM, but balance remains important and excessive joy could cause problems with the heart.
2. Anger – liver: Anger can be detrimental whether it is vented or suppressed. Anger is an interruption in the liver's mission to move and grow. It gives us a tension to propel us forward. The link between feelings of anger and the liver means that remaining in a state of anger frequently or for long periods can disrupt the flow of Qi and cause liver dysfunction.
3. Grief – lung: The lungs are the first line of defense and disperse Qi throughout the body. Unprocessed grief impairs the lung's function and can lead to exhaustion, using up the Qi. According to TCM, our lungs can suffer as a result of experiencing too

much grief, as this emotion can deprive the lungs of vital Qi and deplete the immune system.

4. Worry/overthinking – spleen: Worry is related to the spleen and Earth. Spleen is responsible for transforming food into vital nutrients to the rest of the body. It ensures proper digestive function. Excessive worry and overthinking prohibits the spleen from doing its job. Spleen dysfunction can lead to accumulating fluids and dampness, weighing the body down and leaving it susceptible to more worry. Mindfulness is the best practice to benefit the spleen. The spleen plays an important role in our health by filtering the blood and defending the body against pathogens, but TCM tells us that excessive worry and overthinking can have an adverse effect on the function of the spleen.

5. Fear – kidneys: Kidneys are the core of our constitutional strength. They are the storehouse of jing, which is the genetic material of life. Prolonged fear and sudden fright can deplete the jing and damage the kidney. Experiencing excessive or chronic fear can affect the function of the kidneys, according to TCM.

6. Fright/shock – gallbladder: A person who has suffered a shock or lived through a traumatic experience is often left with high emotions for some time after. TCM tells us this can cause a sudden rise in Qi, causing problems with the health of the gallbladder.

7. Pensiveness/sadness – stomach: In TCM, digestive problems are linked to the emotions of sadness and feeling pensive. Prolonged sadness can stagnate the flow of Qi, affecting the stomach in particular.

Given the way in which emotions and specific organs are linked in TCM, importance is placed on managing emotional well-being in order to maintain a general state of wellness.

Emotional patterns can impress on the body and cause illnesses to manifest in physical form. Although emotions may appear to be immaterial, their impact is made material in the physical body.

When we nurture our spiritual state and pay attention to our emotions, we aid the movement and flow of Qi, lessening the risks of ailments. The Qi helps us protect the body from external pathogens, warms and cools the body, and also holds our organs in place and ensures fluid motion in the body, preventing any stagnations or blockages.

What follows is an illustration of the five ways in which Qi manifests inside the body, also known as the five vital substances:

- **Essence**/jing— Jing can be thought of as the primal energy that carries us through life, making us who we are. It is linked with the physical structure of the body, as well as growth, reproduction and the healthy functioning of major organs.
- **Life force**/ Qi — Qi flows through all matter in the universe, organizing and connecting all things organic and inorganic. Ensuring the flow of Qi around the body promotes health holistically, protecting against pathogens and providing structure, stability and movement.
- **Spirit**/shen — Shen can be thought of as the aspect of our being that is spiritual, and is associated with consciousness and mental health. An imbalance in shen can manifest as psychological illness.
- **Blood**/xue — Xue is energized and activated by Qi, flowing through the blood vessels and in the meridians. Organ health is linked to the flow of xue, as is the maintenance of good mental and emotional well-being.
- **Body fluids**/jinye — TCM separates body fluids into two categories: jin (thin), which are clear and watery fluids for lubrication of the skin and muscles; and ye (thick) which are more viscous and lubricate the joints, brain and spinal cord.

TCM's Holistic Approach

Taoist Chinese Medicine's holistic approach to medicine and patient care is to identify and recognize the whole person as a spiritual, mental, emotional and physical being. This approach emphasizes the interconnectedness of the body, mind and spirit and sees health as a condition of harmony and balance between these facets of the person. To treat the whole person and not a compartmentalized area of illness is the approach taken when working with patients.

The core concept of TCM is to find the root cause of the ailment, and not the isolated source of pain in a problem area. When ailments occur, it is a signal indicating that there is an energy blockage of some sort.

Most Western treatments focus exclusively on the area where symptoms are showing (e.g. the eye), whereas TCM aims to treat the underlying issues of these symptoms, based on the understanding that no part of the body functions in isolation. By integrating multiple types of treatment, TCM aims to restore balance to different systems within the mind, body and spirit.

TCM's Long-Lasting Effects

Western medicine is known to be a "quick fix" modality with short-term benefits, whereas TCM may take longer, but works in a deeper and more holistic manner, producing long-term effects and lasting changes. A simple example of the difference in approach might be a patient experiencing a migraine. Western medicine offers highly effective treatments to reduce the pain of a migraine, whereas TCM would seek to restore balance in the immune system and address the root cause of the migraine.

TCM is Personalized for Patient Needs

Because TCM treats the person and not the symptom, two people experiencing a similar ailment might receive different treatments from a TCM practitioner. This personalized treatment will take into account the individuals symptoms along with their history, their lifestyle, their environment and their body chemistry.

By approaching each patient in this way, TCM not only provides effective care but also helps people to feel seen, listened to and understood, all of which can be important in the healing process.

VI

ORIGIN OF PAIN AND ROOT CAUSES

How do Ailments Start?

Modern society does not know how to slow down.

Exposure to advanced technology and social media are contributing to a dumbing down and numbing of who we are. Our stressful lifestyles and workaholic culture are among the reasons why we are not putting ourselves and our health first. We are overly taxed mentally, emotionally and spiritually, and we are sacrificing our spirits to survive and make money. The way we combat this is to look within.

When you carefully assess your life priorities and value system, you have the opportunity to live in alignment with them. If you value excellent health, would you continue to eat ultra-processed foods and junk foods that offer little nutritional value? Would you work more than 60 hours a week, without taking breaks or getting fresh air and exercise? Would you sacrifice your emotional well-being and your relationships with family & friends?

Overworked Nervous System

Our nervous systems are fried.

When we are constantly on the go and packing our days with non-stop activities or obligations, our nervous system is overloaded and asking for a break. The average American is busy with survival: paying the bills, working overtime 60-70 hours a week just to stay afloat, all while sacrificing their well-being. They let go of their focus on nutrition and regular eating habits. They don't exercise and they are constantly stressed. All perfect ingredients in creating the perfect storm. Stress is the number one culprit in the development of illness.

A certain amount of stress is inevitable in our lives and it is critical that we employ stress management strategies and do everything we can to reduce the impact of stressors in our daily lives. According to the American Psychological Association[8], stress can affect all systems of the body, which means that high levels of stress could lead to everything from respiratory health problems to musculoskeletal issues.

Our autonomic nervous system is comprised of two systems: the sympathetic nervous system (SNS), and the parasympathetic nervous system (PNS). The SNS is responsible for the 'fight or flight' response that takes place in the body when it is under threat. This happens when you're suddenly scared or stressed, prompting adrenaline to be distributed around your body. This is commonly known as an adrenaline rush because it happens so fast. Adrenaline is what gets your body ready to fight or flee danger. However, our bodies are not designed to stay in a state of fight or flight, and this is where issues can arise.

When stress stimulates the sympathetic nervous system, it in turn suppresses the parasympathetic nervous system. The parasympathetic nervous systems regulates the functions of our organs and metabolism and helps us to recover, rest, digest and get into balance.

How We Can Fix and Balance Our Yang and Yin Energies

The way to achieve homeostasis is to calm our nervous system and balance our energies.

In the human body, there are two energy forces: yin and yang. They are the interconnected and opposite forces that exist throughout the natural world, and together they form the whole. Yin and yang are linked to the principle that natural duality affects everything that exists and when this is out of balance, we are out of balance. Stressors in life or any emotional imbalances or negative emotions such as anger, anxiety, and depression can cause our bodies to become unbalanced and trigger a major ailment if not dealt with.

Achieving Balance Through Nutrition: Yin and Yang Foods

When yin and yang are balanced, the body, mind and spirit are balanced. Your internal environment is at peace and harmony. An effective way to balance yourself is to consider eating the right foods for your energetic body type. If you are a person with a hot (yang) body type, it can be helpful to eat yin foods like light salads to achieve balance. If you are a person with a cold (yin) body type, increasing your intake of meat can help to bring fire energy back to your body. Whichever energy force you are deficient in is what you need to eat. As another example, if you have a yang body type, you are yin deficient and therefore need to eat yin foods like Chinese celery, fresh, persimmon, and pork.

For more information on how to eat for your energetic body type, please go to: https://static1.squarespace.com/static/5a11a460f43b5533c014a82c/t/637a6 bbe065b995bb434925d/1668967358318/Fengyang+Taoist+TCM+Diet+ Guide+11-20-2022.pdf

The Interconnectedness of Emotions and The Body

The power of the spirit is an element that most biomedicine and Western doctors do not recognize as a part of their diagnostic procedure. However, TCM treatments create a fertile ground for the spirit to thrive in. TCM treatments help the body open up energy blockages and move the Qi in the proper meridian channels, getting the blood circulating.

The whole-body and holistic approach in Eastern medicine takes into account the potential for ailments and diseases in parts of the body to have been triggered by neighboring organs and systems. Another aspect of this view of interconnectedness is a person's emotional makeup, which is seen as a system in itself and capable of affecting the physical body if emotions are unbalanced. If an individual is harboring negative emotions, these can fester in the body. If a person is failing to take good care of themselves due to feeling sad or stressed, the bad habits that form can begin a trajectory that leads down the rabbit hole.

Positive, balanced emotions can only strengthen the body, the immune system and the mind, and this has a trickle-down-effect on the rest of the body.

Western medicine's approach isolates the condition from the rest of the body and dissects the areas of pain or inflammation and areas of decline in a methodical, almost surgical way. In contrast, Eastern medicine seeks to restore the life force, Qi or energy of the individual by using herbs, ancient modalities, and Taoist Chinese Medicine treatments that help the body regain its balance and vitality.

In many ways the Western and Eastern approaches can be seen as two opposite polarities that view health from completely opposite perspectives, each with their advantages and disadvantages.

By exploring the philosophy of Taoism and gaining an understanding of the Taoist concepts of acceptance, humility, compassion, and yin and yang, we come to see how they contribute to the healing process and how the healing powers of these concepts can be integrated.

Understanding what Tao is and what wholeness means will help us to understand the external and internal causes of sickness and health, such as the foods we eat and the lifestyle we choose.

Practicing Qi Gong or Tai Chi

By practicing Qi Gong or Tai Chi, ancient Chinese martial arts that are similar to light calisthenics, you can actively lower your stress levels. The light movements are designed to move the Qi in the acupuncture meridian channels – passageways through which energy flows around the body – which in turn helps move blood and oxygen throughout the body while releasing tension in the muscles and joints.

The calming and centering effects of practicing Qi Gong or Tai Chi can provide a boost of energy and also strengthen your immune system, reducing the need to lean on less healthy habits for comfort or support.

Identifying the stressors in your life, whether in the areas of work, relationships or personal traumas, and finding ways to manage their impact will have a major bearing on your health as you start to make adjustments and changes that bring more equanimity into your life.

Emotional Health: Reducing Stressors in Life

In the Tao Te Ching, Lao Tzu teaches that the way of Tao is the way of simplicity, humility and harmony with nature. By following this path, one can find inner peace and emotional balance. Just as a tree bends with the wind, Taoism teaches us to be flexible and adaptable in the face of life's challenges. By letting go of our attachment to outcomes and embracing the present moment, we can find freedom from worry and anxiety. Taoism teaches us to cultivate a sense of gratitude and acceptance, appreciating the beauty of each moment and finding joy in the simple things in life. In this way, Taoism can help us find a sense of calm and serenity amidst the turbulence of modern life, allowing us to connect with our true selves and live a more fulfilling and meaningful life. As Paulo Coelho once said: "Happiness is like a butterfly which, when pursued, is always beyond our grasp, but, if you will sit down quietly, may alight upon you."

Know Thyself

In our current modern society, we have lost the connection to ourselves and to the universe and to the Tao, or God, or however you like to name it. We run aimlessly, chasing goals, money, materialism – all in the pursuit of what we think will bring ultimate happiness. We all need to put food on the table and survive, but we find ourselves attempting to address a deeper void inside of us that goes beyond providing for basic needs.

As work, responsibilities and pressures escalate, it is critical to find opportunities to pause and reflect on what we are running so fast towards, and to contemplate the cost of our false pursuit of happiness. Whether you are a high achiever or high performer that just can't seem to relax and be ok with what is and what you already have, or if you are someone on the opposite spectrum who struggles with depression and can't get out of bed and is utterly inactive; there is something going on.

That is the disconnection to oneself and knowing thyself.

We search for external help from medical doctors or gurus who we hope might save us, when the real truth is we need to save ourselves by knowing ourselves and our emotional health, and paying attention to our habits, diet, nutrition, exercise and more.

When we become lost, feel vacuous, or we push too hard at life, life in turn teaches us in ways that signal the body to slow down by giving us pain. Ailments begin, diseases develop. Your higher self and body is screaming at you to get help because you have chosen to neglect it for too long.

When a person truly grasps and understands the Tao and practices Taoism daily and in every moment, it is like returning home. The harmony in oneself in body, mind and spirit becomes aligned and a flow state of consciousness begins. Self-awareness begins. Knowing thyself becomes inevitable.

What is Wu Wei?

Athletes and artists speak about achieving peak performance by entering a "flow state" in which they experience total focus on their task. This occurs through total presence of mind, allowing an individual to truly be in the moment. That flow state is called Tao. Tao is flow. The significance of this way of living is called wu wei, which is effortless being. The egoic self is left on the sidelines while the individual experiences true consciousness and lives from there. There is no need to push, or to exert strength or create any kind of resistance. By harmonizing with Tao, one is just being. Everything becomes easier, effortless and smooth. We begin to flow in life and divine arrangements just happen without us trying. This is the state of mind we associate with great masters, who are experts at entering this realm.

The core truth of healing is wu wei or knowing thyself. We find the answers when we go within and connect with our higher self. When we truly connect with ourselves, we know our own mental, emotional, spiritual and physical conditions, and we become self-aware. When one is self-aware, one knows the truth of one's well-being. We gain access to the root problem that causes the stress that triggers us to do things we would not normally do, or to accumulate the kind of stress level that can eventually lead to hypertension or high blood pressure. How did it all start? The answers are found in knowing thyself.

The practice of wu wei gives us this opportunity to self-reflect and to lean back, observe and not constantly push or pursue. It is observing, seeing, feeling and understanding what is truly important in life, and in this way our actions become the by-product of what we believe in.

Lao Tzu, the ancient philosopher of Taoism, says "the world governs itself". It is we who forcibly interrupt its flow. Allowing things to happen is the motto to adopt. Be one with nature and the flow of nature.

At the opposite end of the spectrum to the Taoist lifestyle is the American "hustle culture". The stereotypical "work hard, play hard" way of life that many Americans aspire to is forcing something that is not ready, creating stress and tension. It is pushing through or powering through when in fact the right thing to do is to just be, and patiently let the universe work things out on its own. When we force, it can lead to ruinous and unwanted results. Let things happen and things get done naturally.

VII

FENGYANG TCM:
THE BEGINNINGS

Dr. Ming Wu, founder and Chinese doctor, Ph.D. of Fengyang Taoist Chinese Medicine adopts this personalized mantra for himself, his students and his patients.

> *I am AIR.*
> *I am LIGHT.*
> *I am WATERFLOW.*

"I am AIR" refers to the oxygen with which we fill up our lungs and the life we breathe. "I am LIGHT" refers to the sunlight that fills us up with energy. "I am WATERFLOW" is the water that opens up all of our body and meridian channels. This mantra represents the principles of our lives and can be used to remind us to connect to ourselves and to nature. We connect to Heaven and Earth with this practice and remember who we are.

To operate and integrate the Taoist spiritual attitude and sentiment is to accept and let go. There is no attachment to anything. There is no attachment to materialism, to people, to status, to power, to money, to achievements or anything at all. It is to become enlightened and to train to oneself to enjoy oneself and the present moment.

When we worry and have too much stress, our physical body and chemistry changes. When we have too much wealth or too many assets, we worry that we will lose our possessions or that they may get stolen. Our present state should not be dictated by or be contingent on external factors. Status or wealth should not dictate how we feel; we should be dictating our internal, emotional makeup and be at peace and harmony within ourselves.

Practicing Taoism: Reducing Stress and Anxiety

By practicing Taoism as described earlier in the chapter, we are able to center ourselves and align with our higher self and to be conscious of everything around us. Essentially, we are in the present moment and harmonizing with the flow of nature and the universe. There is no tension, no struggle, no fight. This state of being seeks only to accept what is, through the model of nature and its cycles.

When we reverse engineer how we got into trouble with ailments and disease in the first place, we find that the root cause is less about genetics and more about the lifestyle, our nutrition, our exercise and personal well-being. It starts with self-analysis, self-awareness and self-responsibility.

Many times we discover that our life priorities are upside-down and that we are not in alignment with what brings us joy, simplicity and excellent health. Diseases start with unchecked emotions and the stress level we are under. A person, for example, that works 60+ hours per week, eating junk food at their desk, pushing through deadlines and not getting up to exercise or take breaks is gradually hurting themselves. The habits of this person accumulate in the body, which hits a tipping point where disease can manifest.

By design, the human body seeks movement and Qi is a huge component in helping the body stay in balance, which can be achieved by keeping the Qi moving in the body through the many meridian channels. When the Qi is blocked, it is like a river with a dam. This can occur as a result of blocked negative emotions, and Qi then becomes an alert system. When Qi moves, blood circulation allows oxygen and nutrients to move as well. The way to achieve this movement is through the ancient martial arts practices of Qi Gong and Tai Chi.

Practicing Qi Gong or Tai Chi is the active, physical form of practicing Taoism. Through these martial art vehicles, we can come to understand ourselves and feel energy in our body. We become aware and truly present, not thinking about tomorrow or yesterday: we are now living in the moment.

The practice of Taoism, Tai Chi or Qi Gong brings our attention back to the self and to knowing who we are. If we know who we are, we are clear and can take action to take care of all aspects of our Being. We take the proper steps to create balance and eat right, exercise right, think right and trust in the laws of nature. There is no anxiety or uncontrollable emotions that can be detrimental to health and happiness. Instead of having to do all the time, we are able to just be.

The Story of Fengyang

Dong Feng, the founder of the Fengyang Chinese Medicine system, lived in Fengyang City on Lu Mountain in China during the Three Kingdoms period (220-280 AD). There, he freely shared many of his powerful secrets on improving personal health and curing diseases with the locals, as many of them were sick and poor. Dong Feng, himself, is said to have lived to over 300 years old. Perhaps it is possible that his practices were able to greatly improve his health and longevity.

Dong Feng, courtesy name Junyi, was born in Houguan (now Minxian in Fujian Province). As a young man, he worked very hard to study the classic works and medicine of China, wanting to become a doctor to help the people. Later on by chance, he met a Taoist monk, who taught him Taoist practices. Not only did he become very skilled in medicine, he could also predict the weather, among other abilities. People regarded him as a celestial being with special powers.

Taoist practices are known to be beneficial in improving one's health and wellness. Dong Feng was able to stay looking young for the rest of his life. According to legend, a young man who was born in the same town first met Dong Feng when he was in his forties. Fifty years later, when he came back to visit his hometown, he saw Dong Feng still looked the same as when they first met. Out of curiosity, he asked Dong Feng: "You were a middle-aged man when I was young. Now my hair has all turned white and you still look the same. Is it because you have achieved the Tao?" Dong Feng answered: "It is just by luck." Throughout history, immortality has been the dream of many emperors and powerful people. When more and more people came to Dong Feng, wanting to get special medicine or to learn practices to achieve immortality, his life was greatly disturbed. He finally left his hometown, and started traveling around the country, helping people with his medical skills.

When he arrived at Jiaozhou (now Guangxi Province), the local governor, Shi Xie, had been in a coma for three days. Dong Feng treated him and nursed him back to health. This news spread quickly to the whole of southern China. Shi Xie and his family were very grateful. They built a tall building by their house for Dong Feng and provided him with delicious food. A year later, Dong Feng declined respectfully of Shi Xie's invitation to stay longer, and continued his travel northward.

When he arrived at Haozhou (now Fengyang in Anhui Province), he saw that the locals were suffering greatly from poverty and diseases due to the war between the three countries. He was sympathetic of their situation, so he decided to settle down in a poor hilly village 18 miles south of the Phoenix Mountain. Considering local geology and weather conditions, he wanted to teach the locals advanced agricultural skills from southern China, and encouraged them to plant apricot trees on the barren mountains to increase income. However, the locals were doubtful because they saw him as just a traveling doctor, and did not want to accept his advice.

Dong Feng thereby announced a rule: he would not charge his patients any money. However, every patient he cured who had a severe illness was asked to plant five apricot trees on the hill next to his house, and every patient with a minor illness plant one apricot tree. Because of his excellent skills and ethics, many patients from near and far came to seek his help. After just a few years, his patients had planted over 10,000 apricot trees. The hill near Dong Feng's house had become an apricot tree woodland. When the apricots ripened, Dong Feng posted a note saying that anyone who wanted to buy apricots could trade one bag of grains for one bag of apricots. He then gave those grains to the poor. It was said that he helped 20-30,000 poor people every year.

During the Three Kingdoms period, Dong Feng's powerful methods became well known in the Fengyang area. The four basic kinds of medicine from Dong Feng are:

1. Fengyang ointment for furuncle (boil),
2. Fengyang medicated liquor for bruise,
3. Fengyang medicinal powder for stopping bleeding,
4. Fengyang Medicine for burns.

Dong Feng's methods were summarized into a system called "Fengyang Health and Wellness Practices and Treatment Methods Using Qi and Pressure Points," which was based on Feng's deep medical knowledge, ancient Taoist teachings and Zen Buddhism practices. It remained in widespread use until the Ming Dynasty many centuries later. Even though many of the locals who practiced these methods were monks and the descendants of the military officers who helped establish the Ming Dynasty, they were suppressed when the new government took over, and could only secretly practice Feng's methods.

After the fall of the Ming Dynasty in 1644, the rulers of the new Qing Dynasty tightened their grip on Fengyang to prevent rebellion. People could still only practice Dong Feng's methods in secret. By the end of the Qing Dynasty in the early 1900s, almost everyone in Fengyang forgot how to practice Dong Feng's ancient healing methods. The practice had almost been entirely destroyed.

Fortunately, some of Feng's disciples moved to what is now called Guangdong Province, where his healing practices were passed down practitioner-to-practitioner, and continued to the present. There it is known as Medicine from Fengyang.[9]

VIII

TREATMENTS OF TCM

Tui Na

Tui Na is an ancient Chinese acupressure massage therapy that utilizes meridian lines to open up Qi. Pressure helps to encourage blood circulation and allows the body to restore homeostasis. Regular Tui Na sessions help to restore the Qi. If there's pain in any area, this is a signal of a blockage, and this is something that Tui Na can help to address.

Fire Cupping

Fire cupping is a treatment that can help to increase energy as toxins are pulled from the body. It involves the warming of glass cups that are used to create suction in areas of a patient's back. The intention is to pull toxins out of the body. This is not a process to be fearful of; its function is to address areas of toxicity. The patient should not experience pain, only pressure caused by the suction pulling and raising the skin.

Qi Gong and Tai Chi

In TCM, Qi Gong and Tai Chi are considered primary practices, dating back to ancient times. By practicing Qi Gong and Tai Chi you can learn to tune into the Tao, the universal force that allows you to be aware of yourself and your surroundings, and to be in touch with nature. The more you practice Qi Gong and Tai Chi, the more attuned you become with the energy force that is all around you. These practices are often prescribed in addition to herbal medicines in order to generate restorative energy in the body. Qi Gong and Tai Chi also help you to release stress and tension, contributing to physical and mental well-being.

Every person's constitution is unique and in TCM, we customize the Chinese herb formula for each person's individual constitution. The process for establishing a person's constitution involves taking a pulse reading and observing the state of the physical body, in order to identify deficiencies and areas in need of attention. While Western medicine applies a fixed prescription based on a symptom, TCM takes into account the individual constitution of each and every patient.

Acupuncture

Acupuncture is one of the most well-known treatments in TCM, and it involves the application of fine needles on points, inserted into the skin around the body in order to balance the flow of Qi. It is used to stimulate the central nervous system that helps release chemicals into the muscles, spinal cord and brain, encouraging biochemical changes that trigger natural healing capabilities. Acupuncture is used when Qi is found to be disrupted or unbalanced, and can be effective in reducing pain and inflammation.

Moxibustion

Moxibustion treatment is carried out by burning plant materials derived from mugwort (Artemisia vulgaris), either directly on the skin or at a distance close to the skin. This treatment aims to promote the flow of blood and unblock the Qi, helping to restore the immune system. People with particular skin conditions, allergies or sensitivity to heat may not be suitable for moxibustion treatment, and a qualified practitioner must be consulted before any treatment is carried out.

Mugwort Footbath

Footbath is a popular modality for people who practice TCM. In China, a mugwort footbath is used to rejuvenate the body and achieve longevity by pulling out toxins. This practice helps to relieve pain, promote circulation and regulate Qi, calming the senses and helping people to age gracefully!

Nutrition

Nutritional guidance for health differs between cultures, and there are disparities between the nutritional guidance provided through TCM and that of Western doctors. For example, it is recommended in TCM that dairy intake is eliminated. In the United States, however, dairy farms have a long history and their produce has become a staple of the American diet. Rather than prescribing a particular diet for all patients, TCM practitioners seek to ascertain the particular constitution of a patient and make dietary recommendations based on their individual characteristics.

IX

HOW WILL AI MEDICINE AFFECT TCM?

It is unquestionable that AI technology is here to stay, and this will ultimately change the entire healthcare landscape and affect the lives of everyone. While the integration of AI into medicine may be of great value in Western medicine, elsewhere it may be a different story.

One of AI medicine's great advantages is it can produce and aggregate a high volume of patient data and medical records for patient analysis in a short time. However, AI can make errors in its fast processing, data collection and generation. If our medical institutions rely heavily only on AI data-generated information, then doctors can be controlled by AI and its decision-making.

AI can be useful, even in herbal medicine. For example, it can provide algorithms that suggest personalized herbal medicine based on a patient's condition. But how can it be seen as preferable for a person to be diagnosed by a computer instead of the personalized human-to-human treatment of TCM? The disparity in ethos and approach between AI medicine and Taoist Chinese Medicine will only bring more attention to the patient care dilemma, and to the processes that are attacking the vital role that human touch between practitioner and patient plays in recovery.

As research and development continues, the machine-learning capabilities of AI will escalate. Given the prominent role AI is likely to play in the collection, storage and use of people's health data, ethical issues must be given due consideration. It must also be kept in mind that the accumulation of data does not equate to expertise.

While AI medicine may seek to gather data on the history of a patient and treat the health pattern it identifies, Taoist Chinese Medicine seeks to understand the unique constitution of each individual's personal needs. AI can recognize health trends and predict potential issues based on a patient's data, but it can never be a substitute for a TCM practitioner or a doctor's diagnosis.

As the concerns and challenges of AI medicine continue to appear, we must ask whether we wish to rely on artificial intelligence or upon natural intelligence that comes from nature itself.

X

THE SPIRITUAL POWER OF TCM

It is beyond doubt that the spiritual component of our bodies and higher selves offer innate healing powers and intelligence from the universe. These faculties are from divinity, constituting the highest art of all creation. Our bodies in essence are designed to heal themselves using innate intelligence and healing properties, given the right composition and environment required in order to thrive. What we think, what we eat and what we do are all doing one of two things: nurturing the self or destroying the self.

The practice of Taoism is to awaken oneself to the universal force and to oneself. Modern society distracts us from our true selves and at this time, it's critical for humanity to return to our true nature that was once pure, righteous and in tune with the Tao, God, or the universal mind. The Qi or vital life force is what keeps us alive. It is the spiritual energy of Tao. As a whole, humankind's culture is disintegrating and withering away with the enormous stresses and declining health of modern life. Work and the pursuit of making money have taken precedence over self-care. Money has triumphed over our true nature. We are neglecting self-care and this is resulting in many diseases and ailments throughout humankind.

When we say to know thyself is the key to knowing who we really are, we are saying that we are not just physical beings. We are spiritual, energetic beings. It starts with the spirit first, then the mind, body and environment follow. It's the ability to know yourself, your body, your emotional makeup, your boundaries and how much you are expending energy throughout various areas of your life. American culture encourages and promotes the "hustle". It is not the natural cycle of life to keep being "ON" and constantly striving to go, go, go!

The yin and yang energies exemplify this delicate balance in everything that we do. When one is off kilter, the body will suffer. If emotions such as anger, resentment, jealousy or any overpowering negative feelings are not dealt with, they can manifest in the body as a Qi blockage, or eventually lead to ailments. Stress has been one of the greatest culprits of disease, creating imbalances of the spirit, mind and body.

The entire concept of Taoist Chinese Medicine (TCM) is that we are part of nature and nature is our model. To understand the model of nature and its cycles, and to connect to it, requires that we harmonize all universal forces. TCM is all about addressing the root cause of where a given ailment started from. We don't just become sick overnight. Something has been trying to tell you through pain, aches or dysfunction that the body is asking for help. Western medicine is a great choice for specific surgical or emergency situations, case by case. Long-term, however, prescriptions are not the answer and only prolong the treadmill of dependency. Taoist Chinese Medicine seeks to make you whole again and independent, to think for yourself and treat yourself. You are your own best doctor and you know how you feel and function day to day, since you live in your own body. The doctor can only observe and diagnose based on what is seen, tested and assessed.

To reduce sickness and suffering, one can adopt Taoism in everyday life as a core practice to keep the spirit, mind and body healthy. By practicing Qi Gong or Tai Chi, we can slow down all aspects of the body and promote balance and Qi flow throughout. Sometimes a spiritual problem can only be resolved using spiritual solutions, and the Taoist lifestyle helps in this manner.

We are at a time in the 21st century when it is important to acknowledge that the current healthcare system is in serious crisis. People are not sheep, put on a treadmill of prescriptions to keep them just alive enough to rake in the billion-dollar profits of pharmaceutical companies. The medical system is more concerned with profit than people and some medical doctors aren't intentionally seeking to resolve your issues, when there is money to be made by sending you for more MRI scans and x-rays, and to see more specialists. Vital communication exchanges between specialists and primary doctors are often lost in translation. Collaboration is breaking down. In other cases, patients have been confidently diagnosed by their traditional and conventional doctors and prescribed with specific treatments or drugs, and yet they are not getting better – sometimes worse. This is when we need to ask: where is the root cause and are we really addressing it?

We are at a crossroads.

Many individuals find value in combining both Western medicine and Taoist Chinese Medicine (TCM). This is known as integrative or complementary medicine, where Western medicine is used for acute conditions and Chinese medicine for chronic conditions or overall wellness. Ultimately, each one of us seeks a quality of life with less suffering.

However, the purpose of this book is to offer the alternative option of TCM when nothing else is working after years of treatment within the Western approach. The goal is to demonstrate that there is another option for healthcare and well-being.

By taking your power back and knowing yourself and how you truly feel, you can make new choices in your medical care that can improve your health and nourish your well-being. There are many real life case studies demonstrating the work of Dr. Ming Wu (Ph.D.), from Fengyang Taoist Chinese Medicine. In the pages that follow, we invite you to review real life stories and how these patients recovered fully by choosing Taoist Chinese Medicine (TCM) to address their ailments.

The spiritual approach of TCM is how we address and fix the root cause of any ailment. When we integrate our lives with the Tao, God and the universal mind, we are in touch with ourselves and with nature. We are living in the Tao, which is effortless living. This kind of lifestyle eliminates force, stress and constant adrenaline, and promotes the ability to just be and to trust our own intuition. Our own intuition speaks the truth, knows the truth and lives the truth. Connect with the Tao in everything you do, and it no longer becomes compartmentalized; it then becomes all of you.

Case Studies

Case study: snake bite

Patient: male, 66 years old

Symptoms: patient's right hand was bitten by a poisonous snake in June 2019. The patient was admitted to a TCM hospital in China, then transferred to the intensive care unit of another hospital 2 days later. He was again transferred to a different hospital 3 days later. He was discharged 12 days later. At the time of discharge, his right hand was swollen with a quarter-sized wound. At home, he took oral medicine, plus medicinal hand wash and external ointment. A month after being discharged, the wound was still not healed. It was red and swollen, with pus oozing out.

Dr. Wu's prescription:

1. TCM formula
   Zao jiao ci 10g, huang qi 60g, chen pi 10g, lian qiao 10g, sheng ma) 10g, dang shen 10g, gan cao 5g, dang gui 10g, chai hu 15g, wu zhi mao tao 30g, gui zhi 10g. Drink the concoction once a day for five days.

2. Moxibustion treatment on the wound for 20 minutes a day.
   Ten days later, the patient's wound was almost completely healed.

Before treatment:	After treatment:	Healing process:

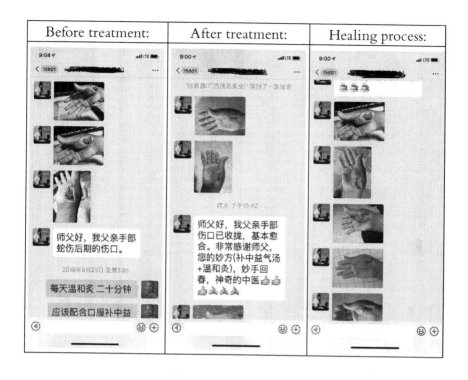

Case study: a good example of changes in tongue after TCM treatment

Patient: female

Symptoms: lower extremity joint swelling and pain for two years, fatigue.

Chinese medicine diagnosis: weak spleen, pale tongue, and thick coating.

Dr. Wu's prescription, August 2016:

Gui zhi 10g, cang zhu 10g, huai niu qi 10g, mu gua 10g, wei ling xian 10g, ji xue teng 20g, niu da li 20g, qian jin ba 10g, ci diao gen 10g, wu duo nian 10g, dang gui 10g, dang shen 10g, fu ling 10g, bai zhu 10g, gan cao 5g, wu zhua long 20g.

Decoction, one dose a day, five consecutive doses.

Before treatment:	After treatment:

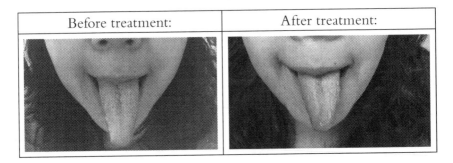

Follow-up 5 days later: symptoms alleviated, five more doses using the original formula.

Case study: hepatitis C

Patient: female

Date of first visit: March, 2005

Chief complaints: pain in the side.

Hospital diagnosis: hepatitis C. The patient was cross-infected after getting an eyebrow tattoo at a beauty center.

TCM diagnosis: string pulse, red tongue, yellow moss.

Dr. Wu's prescription: chuan dong zi 10g, chai hu 10g, ze lan 10g, ban lan gen 15g, da qing ye 10g, mai dong 10g, peony skin 10g, ban zhil ian 10g, ling zhi 6g, dried tangerine peel 10g, boil in water, drink the liquid, one dose per day, a total of 52 doses.

Follow-ups: one year later, patient said hospital test found no signs of hepatitis C. Another follow-up in 2019, patient said there has been no recurrence since.

Case study: jaundice hepatitis

Patient: male, 17 years old

Chief complaints: The patient was diagnosed with jaundice hepatitis in 2004. He was hospitalized for a week, but had no improvement.

Dr. Wu suggested that he be discharged immediately to prevent nosocomial infection.

Dr. Wu's prescription: chai hu 10g, yin chen 30g, da huang 10g, zhi shi 10g, mai ya 10g, dan shen 10g, ze lan 10g, ban zhi lian 10g, wild ling zhi 30g, fu ling 10g, gan cao 5g. One dose a day for 10 consecutive days.

After taking the herbal prescription, the patient's symptoms all disappeared. Hospital check-up exam results were all normal.

Study case: high blood pressure

Patient: female, 70 years old

Date of first visit: May 2015

Chief complaints: patient suffered from high blood pressure and hyperlipidemia for five years. Western medicine's side effects caused liver and kidney damage, systemic joint pain, systemic muscle pain, both ankle joints swelling, and insomnia. Her daughter-in-law (a Western internal medicine doctor) suggested that she should come to see Dr. Wu.

TCM diagnosis: pulse wiry, tongue dark red, coating greasy and yellow.

TCM syndrome differentiation: kidney yin deficiency, excess liver yang.

TCM treatment: Tui Na and cupping.

TCM prescription: ancient tree pu-erh tea (2009 raw tea) 10g per day to make tea, drink about 500ml of tea per day; plus 500mg of wild ling zhi powder, 500g of organic cinnamon powder, and 500g of wild kuding tea per day to take orally. Stop eating dairy products and wheat products, reduce meat intake, eat brown rice and more vegetables.

Patient feedback: on the second day, the patient's blood pressure dropped from 155/95 to 137/79. The patient stopped taking all Western medicines. On the fifth day, the patient's blood pressure dropped to 119/80. The whole body pain completely disappeared, the ankle edema disappeared, and sleep was completely normal. Dr. Wu suggested the patient to practice Tai Chi twice a week, one hour each time. Two months later, the patient had Tui Na and cupping treatments three times; she had good energy, good sleep quality, and was feeling rejuvenated. She was enjoying life, and thanked God every day for Chinese medicine. She introduced several of her friends to come and see Dr. Wu.

Case study: kidney stone

Patient: male, 64 years old

Date of first visit: July 2016

Chief complaints: patient experienced abdominal pain, nausea, vomiting. Emergency room CT results: kidney stone, 0.5cm in diameter. TCM treatment:

1. Jinqiancao 60g, boil in two cups of water until the liquid is reduced to one cup. Drink the liquid. Repeat once a day for seven days.
2. Cupping and Tui Na.

First follow-up appointment: July 2016

Patient reported the abdominal pain has lessened. An appointment was made for him to have surgery later in the month.

TCM treatment:

1. Ask the patient to practice abdominal breathing method for one hour per day.
2. Tui Na and cupping.
3. Herbal medicines to make tea.

Herbal medicine formula:

Guangjinqiancao 30g, jinqiancao 10g, mutong 10g, tongcao 5g, muxiang 10g, cheqianzi 10g, zhuling 10g, tufuling 20g, rue 5g.

First boil all the herbs in four cups of water until the liquid is reduced to two cups. Drain the liquid to drink. Boil the remnant in three cups of water to make another two cups of tea. Repeat once a day for seven days.

Second follow-up appointment: July 2016

Patient found the kidney stone came out during urination at 1am that morning. He cancelled his appointment for surgery.

Case study: chronic diarrhea

Patient: male, 29 years old

Date of first visit: Nov 2015

Chief complaints: frequent diarrhea and pain at lower abdomen. Patient often had diarrhea several times a day, and no improvement after many treatments.

TCM diagnosis: pulse deep and fine, tongue pale red, and coating white and greasy.

TCM syndrome differentiation: spleen and stomach deficiency-cold, exuberant dampness.

TCM prescription: huo xiang 10g, hou pu 15g, su ye 10g, da fu pi 10g, dang shen 20g, fu ling 10g, gan cao 3g, chao bai zhu 30g, wu zhu long 10g, sheng jiang 5g. Take 20 consecutive doses.

First follow-up date: Dec. 2016. Patient's symptoms improved significantly. In the past, he had diarrhea several times a day, but now his stool is a bit shaped. He has bowel movements once or twice every few days, and the abdominal pain has disappeared.

TCM prescription: dang shen 30g, fu ling 20g, chao bai zhu 30g, zhi gan cao 5g, wu zhu mao tao 20, chen pi 5g, gan jiang 5g, huang qi 20g, huo xiang 10g, hou pu 15g, su ye 10g, da fu pi 10g, jie geng 5g, shen qu 10g, rou gui 3g, ling zhi bo zi powder 3g, wild American ginseng powder 1g, one dose per day, 20 consecutive doses.

Case study: pityriasis rosea

Chief complaints: red and very itchy rash on the back, abdomen and thigh areas for two weeks. The patient was diagnosed with pityriasis rosea by a dermatologist who believed that the cause was unknown and that there was no cure.

Date of first visit: Nov 2005

TCM diagnosis: floating pulse, tongue light red, coating thin and white.

TCM treatment principle: expel wind and detoxify to itching.

TCM prescription:

1. She tui 6g, chan tui 6g, bai xian pi 10g, ban lan gen 15g, fang feng 6g, qiang huo 6g, xu chang qing 6g. To make decoction, one dose a day, five consecutive doses.
2. Hibiscus tincture applied externally, twice a day.

The patient's symptoms disappeared after five days of treatment.

Follow-up date: Oct. 2015. No recurrence so far.

Case study: perianal inflammation

Chief complaints: patient suffered from perianal inflammation with a large thumb-sized lump and strong pain for a few days. Doctor at the hospital told him after the exam that as long as the inflammation and lump went away, there was no need for surgery. The doctor told the patient to take anti-inflammatory injections and medicines. The patient didn't want the treatment, so he sought Dr. Wu for help.

Date of first visit: Oct. 2015

TCM prescription: chuan shan jia 6g, tian hua powder 10g, dang gui 10g, jin yin hua 10g, lian qiao 15g, zao jiao ci 20g, ci diao gen 15g, chi shao 10g, ru xiang 10g, mo yao 10g, pu gong ying 10g, zi hua di ding 10g, da huang 10g, gan cao 6g, chen pi 10g, zhe bei mu 10g, fried lai fu zi 20g. To make decoction, one dose a day for five consecutive doses.

Patient feedback: after three doses, the pain was almost gone. After taking two more doses, the lump has mostly disappeared. The patient is still taking the medicine and hopes to recover soon.

Case study: colitis

Patient: male, 41 years old

Chief complaints: patient had colon disease for nearly four years. Rectal ulcers, erosions and bloody stools. Patient sought medical treatments at several hospitals, but the condition was not improved.

TCM prescription: hou pu 10g, su ye 10g, da fu pi 10g, jie gen 10g, dang shen 10g, fu ling 10g, fried bai zhu 10g, gan cao 3g, huo xiang 10g, to make decoction, one dose per day for 20 consecutive doses.

Patient feedback: the bleeding has stopped, and the patient is feeling much better.

Case study: cervical and thoracic vertebrae demyelinating

Patient: female, 64 years old

Chief complaints: left lower limb weakness accompanied by swelling and soreness for three years. Patient couldn't walk when the situation was severe.

Hospital diagnosis: cervical and thoracic vertebrae demyelinating and left lower limb venous thrombosis. Patient has been taking oral hormones and immunosuppressive drugs for three years. Patient's situation was sometimes good and sometime bad, and showed strong hormone dependence.

TCM diagnosis: dark tongue, obvious dark blood stasis spots on tip and sides of the tongue, and greasy white coating.

TCM syndrome differentiation: spleen and stomach deficiency, blood stasis obstructing the meridians.

TCM treatment principle: mainly tonify the spleen, supported by promoting blood and qi circulation.

TCM prescription: huang qi 60g, wu zhua long 60g, bai zhu 30g, sheng ma 10g, chai hu 10g, dang shen 30g, chen pi 10g, zhi gan cao 6g, zhi chuan wu 6g, dang gui 15g, di long 10, ji xue teng 20g, to make decoction. Take for five consecutive days.

Patient feedback: when drinking Chinese medicine, the patient gradually reduced the amount of hormone intake until she stopped taking it completely. Ten days later, patient reported that the skin color of the leg became normal, having been redder before. The leg felt lighter, and the mobility was better. The leg paralysis situation was also improved.

Case study: heatstroke

Patient: female, 58 years old

Chief complaints: chills and fever, severe diarrhea, syncope, sleepiness, fatigue, repeated symptoms for two months.

TCM diagnosis: tongue red, coating white and greasy, pulse rapid and soggy. Symptoms belong to the category of heat and dampness.

TCM treatment principles: dispel wind and clear heat, eliminate dampness through body's surface.

TCM prescription: xiang ru cao 10g, chuan hou pu 10g, bai bian dou 10g, hua shi fen 30g, gan cao 6g.

Patient feedback: diarrhea stopped after three doses.

Doctor's recommendation: Tui Na on hua tuo jia ji T1-3 and T11, plus moxibustion on ST36 and ST37 to stabilize the effects.

Case study: Lyme disease

Patient: female, 50 years old

Date of first visit: Jan 2015

Chief complaints: joint pain in the whole body, muscle spasms, ataxia, severe fatigue. Patient was diagnosed with Lyme disease three years earlier.

TCM diagnosis: spleen pulse weak, liver pulse choppy, tongue pale and dim, coating thin and white.

TCM syndrome differentiation: liver Qi stagnation, dampness and spleen deficiency.

TCM treatment principle: soothing liver and regulating Qi, strengthening spleen and clear dampness.

TCM prescription: chai hu10g, wu zhu mao tao 30g, ci diao gen 10g, bai hua shi mu tou gen 10g, bai zhi 10g, zi su ye 10g, gui zhi 10g, qian jin ba 10g, sang zhi 20g, fu ling 30g, zhi ban xia 6g, shen qu 10g, chao bai zhu 30g, chen pi 10g, hou pu 10g, huo xiang 10g, gan cao 6g, to make a decoction, one dose every two days for 14 consecutive doses.

Tui Na treatment: hua tuo jia ji xue C2, T1, 2, 3, 7. One hour each time, two times per week, for eight times total.

Dr. Wu's note: the initial diagnosis of this case required two hours, one hour for pulse diagnosis and other TCM syndrome differentiation treatment and TCM psychological counseling, and one hour for Tui Na treatment. By the fourth follow-up visit four weeks later, the patient's clinical symptoms had basically disappeared, the patient recovered to the physical condition of 20 years earlier, and their quality of life is completely normal. I generally encouraged the patient to live in the present, let go of labels (remove the original Western medicine diagnosis effect). Living in the moment is powerful.

The conventional Western medicine treatment for Lyme disease is antibiotics. Patients with severe case can take oral antibiotics for up to two years. Those to whom the treatment is not effective are then diagnosed with chronic Lyme disease (Western medicine considers diseases against which Western treatment is ineffective as incurable diseases). They do not give patients any hope. This is why I work with the patient to remove the Western medicine labels, because these labels are like a curse that kills the patient.

For patients with cancer, AIDS, hepatitis, or any other serious and chronic diseases, the doctor and patient must be in the present to remove the labels during the first appointment. Chinese medicine calls this "same treatment for different diseases". The curative effect of doctors and patients working together requires the credibility and personal brand established by the doctors in the community.

When working with hospitals and any Chinese and Western medicine groups, Chinese medicine experts should retain their personal brand and adhere to the principles of Tao and nature. Every day when doing consultation and treatment, a doctor should always live in the state of meditation. I conducted an experiment with a Western medicine expert. When I walked into the consultation room, an electrocardiogram was performed on me. One can see the obvious changes in the electrocardiogram. When I entered the room, I entered a state of deep meditation. This also explains why this Lyme disease patient trusted me after only two hours at our first appointment. These patients are more sensitive to energy and can immediately feel the positive energy when they are in contact with you. *The Yellow Emperor's Inner Canon* said: "When there is sufficient vital Qi inside, pathogenic factors have no way to invade the body."

Case study: severe headache

Patient: female, 35 years old

Date of first visit: Feb 2007

Chief complaints: headache for two days. The patient was exposed to wind on her way home. She had severe headache one hour after arriving home. The headache came and went for two days.

TCM diagnosis: pulse floating, tongue light pink, coating thin and yellow.

TCM syndrome differentiation: yangming headache.

TCM prescription: qing zhen tang (he ye 30g, cang zhu 20g, sheng ma 10g).

Patient feedback: headache was gone after one dose.

Follow-up in Oct. 2013: there was no relapse.

Case study: blastocystis hominis parasite

Patient: female, 65 years old

Date of first visit: Oct. 2012

Chief complaints: abdominal pain and diarrhea for four weeks, defecation five times a day. Patient was diagnosed with human blastocystis chronic enteritis by fecal examination.

TCM diagnosis: pulse wiry, tongue pale, coating thin and white.

TCM treatment principle: clear dampness and kill the parasites.

TCM prescription: jin jie 10g, chai hu 10g, cang er zi 6g, gui zhi 15g, shi jun zi 6g, qian jin ba 15g, fu ling 10g, ren dong teng 15g, chuan dong zi 6g. To make decoction. One dose per day for 10 days.

First follow-up date: Oct. 2013. Abdominal pain and diarrhea disappeared after 10 days. Fecal examination result is normal.

Case study: stomach flu

Patient: male, 1 year old

Date of first appointment: Jan 2008

Chief complaints: nausea and vomiting, diarrhea, chills and fever for one day.

TCM diagnosis: pulse floating.

TCM prescription: xiang ru cao 6g, hou pu 6g, bai bian dou 10g, hua shi fen 20g, gan cao 3g, to make decoction.

Patient feedback: the symptoms disappeared one hour after drinking the decoction.

Case study: infant rash

Patient: male, 6.5 months old

Chief complaints: fever, bloating and constipation six days earlier. After inducing bowel movement, the fever is gone. However, now he defecates as soon as he eats. Four days ago, a red rash appeared all over his body.

TCM treatment: boiling da huang 10g and lian qiao 20g to make a bath, plus using fengyang hand, foot and mouth. Chinese medicine powder paste on yongquan acupressure point.

Patient feedback: the patient slept well that night. The heat rash obviously got better the next day, and on the third day, it basically disappeared.

Case study: myasthenia gravis

Patient: male, 37 years old

Chief complaints: Patient could barely open one of his eyes. He had trouble walking up a hill or carrying anything more than 10 pounds.

TCM diagnosis: spleen and stomach Qi deficiency.

TCM prescription: wu zhua long 50g, huang qi 60g, dang shen 30g, chao bai zhu 30g, chen pi 10g, sheng ma 10g, chai hu 10g, zhi gan cao 5g, dang gui 10g.

Other TCM treatment: moxibustion for one hour a day, mugwort foot bath, abdominal breathing, fengyang Qi Gong.

Patient feedback: patient felt significantly better after seven days. After two months, most of his motor functions are backed, and he can open both eyes.

Case study: chronic joint pain

Patient: female

Chief complaints: lower extremity joint swelling and pain for two years, fatigue easily.

TCM diagnosis: spleen pulse weak, tongue pale, coating greasy.

TCM prescription: gui zhi 10g, cang zhu 10g, huai niu qi 10g, mu gua 10g, wei ling xian 10g, ji xue teng 20g, niu da li 20g, qian jin ba 10g, ci diao gen 10g, wu duo nian 10g, dang gui 10g, dang shen 10g, fu ling 10g, bai zhu 10g, gan cao 5g, wu zhua long 20g. To make decoction. One dose a day for five consecutive days.

Patient feedback: patient's symptoms have lessened. Patient's tongue diagnosis results are much better.

Case study: aortic valve insufficiency, tricuspid insufficiency, and mitral regurgitation

Patient: male, 41 years old

Date of first visit: May 2020

Chief complaints: chest tightness, paralysis, aphasia, difficulty opening mouth, paralysis of the limbs, fatigue of the whole body, unable to walk for more than an hour. Hospital diagnosis: aortic valve insufficiency, tricuspid insufficiency and mitral regurgitation.

TCM diagnosis: pulse thin and choppy, tongue dark red with obvious blood stagnation spots, coating yellow and greasy.

TCM syndrome differentiation: stagnant liver Qi, stagnant Qi and blood.

TCM treatment:

1. Acupuncture and Tui Na treatment.
2. TCM prescription: huang qi 80g, dang gui wei 10g, chi shao 10g, di long 10g, chuan xiong 5g, hong hua 10g, tao ren 10g, zhen di gen 10g, ji xue teng 10g. To make decoction, one dose a day for three consecutive days. Plus san qi powder 3g, to take with water, twice a day for three days.

First follow-up date: 3 days later

TCM treatment:

1. Acupuncture and Tui Na treatment once a day for 10 consecutive days
2. 99% vegetarian diet, no alcohol, no dairy, no rich food such as meat and fish.
3. TCM prescription: huang qi 60g, dang gui wei 10g, chi shao 10g, di long 6g, chuan xiong 5g, hong hua 10g, tao ren 10g, xi huang cao 10g, da huang 6g, zhi shi 10g, ze xie 10g, dan shen

10g, chai hu 10g, gua lou pi 10g, jiu bai 3g, qian hu 6g, ji geng 3g. To make decoction, one dose a day for five consecutive days. Plus san qi powder 3g, to take with water, twice a day for five days.

4. Green rhyme cell physiotherapy quantum machine one hour per day for 10 consecutive days.

Case study: kidney yang collapse and stomach stroke

Patient: female, 37 years old

Date of first visit: April 2020

Chief complaints: extreme weakness, unable to eat or drink, dizziness, cold stomach, acid reflux.

TCM syndrome differentiation: deficiency of spleen and kidney yang.

TCM treatment: warming the spleen and stomach, invigorating kidney yang.

TCM prescription: wuzhuyu decoction + zhenwu decoction + buzhong yiqi decoction.

Note: When Dr. Wu first started to treat the patient, she had already been unable to eat for six weeks. She even had trouble swallowing water. The patient was depending on IV and oxygen to maintain life. The world-class hospital in Thailand was not able to help her, so she asked Dr. Wu to have a remote consultation. Since she could not eat or drink, Dr. Wu prescribed a herbal mixture for external use (stick in the belly button and the yongquan point (K1), combined with gentle moxibustion along GV and CV. After 24 hours, the patient can drink water and Chinese medicine. She was able to eat porridge and was discharged from the hospital after two weeks.

The patient still had difficulty breathing when being discharged from the Thai International Hospital. Her breathing function was at level 3.

The patient continued to take Chinese medicine for five months (zhenwu decoction, buzhong yiqi decoction, wendan decoction, and xiao yao san, etc.) to tonify the spleen and stomach, disperse stagnated liver Qi for relieving Qi stagnation, to remove phlegm and improve gallbladder functions. Along with acupuncture treatments, the patient's breathing function has improved from level 3 to 7.

In Sept. 2020, the patient had skin rashes all over her body, the itching was unbearable. The Thailand dermatologist diagnosed that she had psoriasis and recommended oral prednisone. Because of the patient's past negative experience with steroids, she was unwilling to use it again. Dr. Wu held a consultation with Dr. Zhang Ni. Their TCM diagnose is: cold and dampness blocking the middle burner, and stagnation of liver and Qi. Dr. Zhang Ni prescribed a decoction to strengthen the spleen, dissolve dampness, and sooth the liver and regulate Qi. The patient took the decoction for two weeks, both orally and as a washing liquid. The rash completely disappeared, and her breathing function also improved from level 7 to 9.

Case study: hearing loss

Patient: female

Date of first visit: April 2020

Chief complaint: loss of 80% hearing in one ear, and phlegm in throat. The pulse is thin and choppy, and the tongue is pale and greasy.

TCM diagnosis: deafness due to wind–phlegm blocking orifice (inner ear labyrinth obstruction caused by stroke sequelae).

TCM treatment: dispelling wind and phlegm and opening orifices, promoting blood circulation and dredging collaterals, invigorating spleen, invigorating Qi and dispelling dampness.

TCM prescription: huang qi 50g, dang gui 20g, ji xue teng 20g, chuan xiong 10g, chi shao 10g, di long 10g, hong hua 10g, tao ren 10g, gui zhi 10g, dan shen 10g, zhi tian nan xing 10g, bei mu 10g, gua lou 10g, shi chang pu 10g, jin jie 10g, chai hu 10g, cang zhu 10g, yi yi ren 10g, fu ling 10g.

Patient feedback: Symptoms (deafness) disappeared within an hour of drinking the herbal decoction.

Case study: COVID-19 recovery

Patient: female

Date of first visit: Nov 2021

Chief complaint: seven days after catching COVID-19, the patient had sore throat, thick phlegm, cough, no appetite, trouble taking food, and was feeling tired.

TCM diagnosis: spleen and kidney pause weak. Tongue color pale with thin white coating. Teeth mark on edge of tongue.

TCM prescription: dang shen 10g, fu ling 10g, bai zhu 10g, ban xia qu 10g, wu zhu long 20g, gan cao 6g, chen pi 6g, fa ban xia 6g, su geng 10g, cang zhu 10g, chao gu ya 10g, chao mai ya 10g, da zao 2 pieces. Five packages for five days.

Date of second appointment: Dec. 2022

Chief complaint: night sweating for one month, sweat wet the clothes at the neck, chest, and back areas.

TCM prescription: huang qi 60g, chao bai zhu 20g, fang feng 10g. Three packages for three days.

Patient feedback: night sweating stopped after three days.

Case study: neck back to chest pain

Patient: female, 61 years old

Date of first visit: June 2022

Chief complaints: neck, back pain that goes to the chest. Limited neck mobility.

Tongue diagnosis: pale and fat tongue, thick and white coating, clear teeth marks.

TCM syndrome differentiation: Qi and blood deficiency, cold and dampness blocking the channels.

TCM diagnosis:

1. Cold and dampness type Bi Zheng (obstruction syndrome)
2. Xiong Bi (thoracic obstruction)

Treatment principles: tonify and invigorate blood, expel cold and dampness, clear and activate channels.

TCM prescription: chuan shan long 10g, ge gen 10g, ci diao gen 10g, ji xue tang 20g, dan shen 10g, ze lan 10g, chi shan 10g, fu ling 10g, gui zhi 10g, pei lan 10g, hu zhang 10g, sang zhi 10g.

Follow up: after five doses of the TCM formula, patient no longer has pain in the neck, back and chest region. Her neck mobility has been restored.

Case study: head and neck cancer

Patient: female, 34 years old

Date of first visit: Dec 2020

Chief complaint: tongue cancer, head and neck cancer, recurring after one year of surgery, chemotherapy and radiotherapy. Pale tongue, white and greasy coating, deep and weak spleen and kidney pulse.

TCM treatment:

1. Aconite powder 1g, evodia powder 1g, mix well with huo xiang zheng qi san to form a paste. Put paste in belly button (CV8).
2. Tui Na plus cupping for one hour.
3. Herbal powder mixture to take orally for 30 days.
4. Tangerine white tea. Ten grams to make tea to drink every day.

TCM prescription: pueraria 10g, coix seed 20g, gorgon fruit 10g, jujube 10g, licorice 10g, lotus seed 10g, ganoderma lucidum 10g, turtle shell 10g, astragalus 10g, turmeric 10g, schisandra 10g, bupleurum 10g, smilax 10g, poria cocos 20g, huoxiang 10g, evodia 10g, codonopsis 10g, atractylodes macrocephala 10g, baishao 10g, paofuzi 30g, suanzaoren 10g, dried ginger 10g, bombyx silkworm 10g, keel 10g, polygala 10g.

Take three grams each time, dissolved in four ounces of warm water, two times a day for a total of 30 days.

Dr. Wu also asked the patient to stop consuming milk products, soybean products and other cold and phlegm-damp causing foods, and to practice Qi Gong every day, combining movement and stillness.

At the end of Dec 2022, the patient went to the cancer hospital for physical examination, and the result was negative, and there was no recurrence in two years. The oncologist believes that the patient does not need to have an annual oncology examination anymore. Dr. Wu encouraged the patient to continue practicing Qi Gong, and to continue to eat healthy and enjoy life.

Case study: athlete's foot (fungal infection)

Patient: male

Date of first visit: Feb 2023

Chief complaint: athlete's foot (fungal infection). The toe is itchy and swollen for seven days, and has suppurated. The local Chinese medicine clinic prescribed TCM for oral administration, and dexamethasone ointment for external application, combined with antibiotics (cephalosporin) orally, but the condition worsened every day.

Dr. Wu recommended to stop all Western medicines and use only TCM for oral administration and to soak the feet. The swelling and pain mostly disappeared in one day.

TCM prescription:

1. ku shen 50g, huang bai 20, lian qiao 20g, da huang 30g, boil in water to make a wash. Soak feet once a day.
2. Bao yi san, take orally four capsules for three times a day.
3. Apply compound hibiscus bark tincture once on infected areas.

Credits and Acknowledgments

Jason Ni

Wei Li

Sources:

- Tao Te Jing
- https://www.sitcm.edu.au/blog/Qi-and-the-five-vital-substances-in-tcm-fundamentals/)
- https://yinyanghouse.com/theory
- https://www.sitcm.edu.au/blog/why-chinese-medicine-simply-works/

Citations

[1] https://news.gsu.edu/research-magazine/can-americas-healthcare-crisis-be-solved

[2] https://www.cnbc.com/2020/12/16/covid-vaccine-side-effects-compensation-lawsuit.html

[3] https://pubmed.ncbi.nlm.nih.gov/31975898/

[4] https://plato.stanford.edu/entries/chinese-phil-medicine/

[5] https://www.rand.org/news/press/2021/01/28.html

[6] https://www.cbo.gov/publication/57126

[7] https://www.ncbi.nlm.nih.gov/pmc/articles/PMC4203477/

[8] https://www.apa.org/topics/stress/body

[9] Reproduced with permission from https://wuhealing.com/

About the Authors

About Dr. Ming Wu, Ph.D.

 Dr. Ming Wu (Ph.D.), is a doctor of Chinese Medicine and a 20th-generation Fengyang Taoist Chinese Medicine practitioner, the only one teaching in the United States. He is also a highly accomplished Master Qi Gong and Tai Chi practitioner with over 40 years of experience studying and teaching in China and the United States.

Wu was born and grew up in Wu Village in Chaozhou. [1] In 1986, he received his TCM doctor license and worked for Chaozhou Hospital to practice TCM in orthopedics. In 1994, he received his doctorate in TCM. With over 20 editorials published in Chinese Medical Journal, he is recognized in The Annals of China's Contemporary Famous Doctors of TCM. He also studied the true tradition of ancient Chinese medicine in the lineage of Dr. Dong Feng and Dr. Deng Tietao.

Wu's Career in Chinese Medicine began at the age of 7 when he started training with his father, Mu Qing. With over 33 years of experience, Wu has taught students in the United States Qi Gong and Tai Chi.

Wu started his medicine career in the Orthopedic Traditional Chinese Medicine (TCM) department of Chao Zhou Hospital, China, where he developed his diagnostic skills, It was during this period that he first encountered therapeutic potential of Fengyang TCM.

His interest in preserving the ancient wisdom of Fengyang TCM, Wu established the Wu Healing Center in Puning, Guangdong, China, back in 1987, He expanded his practice by founding the Taoist Institute of TCM and Wu Healing Center in Massachusetts and Connecticut, USA, in 1989.

He also studied under Yang Style Tai Chi instruction from his Sifu Grandmaster Gin Soon Chu, who was a disciple of Yang Sau Chung. He has also received Tong Ren Therapy Certification and training from Master Tom Tam since 1994.

He recently starred in the documentary "Who Am I," which aims to promote Chinese medicine health and wellness practices.

About Judy Lin:

Judy Lin is the founder/CEO of Digital Marketing Doctor Agency, a boutique digital marketing agency based in Carlsbad, CA, where she lives. For over 20 years she has worked with start-ups, established corporate accounts and private medical practices.

Judy graduated with a bachelor's degree in English with a writing emphasis from the University of San Francisco. She also attended USF on a collegiate tennis scholarship, playing Division I. In her free time, she enjoys being an artist in all mediums and is now a sculptor. Her other hobbies include tennis, pickleball, SUP, yoga, Qi Gong, writing and meditation.

Printed in the United States
by Baker & Taylor Publisher Services